Falls from Grace, Favor and High Places

By Philip M. Butera

Philip Butera

JaCol Publishing Inc.

FIRST PRINTING

September 2021

JaCol Publishing Inc.

195 Murica Aisle

Irvine, CA 92614

818-510-2898

ISBN: **978-1-946675-61-3**

Books by

Philip M. Butera

Poetry:

Mirror Images and Shards of Glass

Dark Images at Sea

I Never finished Loving You

Novels:

Caught Between

Art and Mystery: The Lost Poe Manuscript (Available Fall
2021 by Jacol Publishing)

Play:

The Apparition

Cover Design---Chris Moore

Southern Printing---www.southernprintingandmarketing.net

Cover Photo:---Colin Dixon

Website colindixonphotography.co.uk

Instagram @malmesburyportraits

Model: Selkie---Instagram @selkie_model

Preface

Philip Butera never fails to stun his many readers. This volume is no exception. His brilliance makes this the book that lingers on the desk or coffee table, teasing the reader with "just once more." Each reading offers more to ingest and digest. His knowledge of the classics and the skillful manner that he weaves them into modern storylines is impressive in various poetic forms. He is fluent in romance without a catalog of butterflies and rainbows. Instead, he cuts precisely into the meat of loving and loss.

There is little unsaid. Philip sees no reason to cauterize the true nature of relationships gone awry but maintains that memory seldom serves as a salve. This book is a testament to the fact that poetry walks, runs, and gallops through our lives and is intrinsic to our truly grasping the entirety of human existence.

When Philip Butera and Lorna Thomson write together, their juxtaposition- male and female perspectives of love and loss braid us through realities with language distinct and without shadows. These pieces are lovely and easily offer the reader an understanding of the roles we often play in concert.

Falls from Grace, Favor and High Places is a remarkable book of poetry.

Kathleen Bryce Niles–Overton, Editor, Comstock Review

THE BRYCE FOCUS GROUP

kathleenbryceniles.com

Praise for Philip Butera's Poetry

"Philip Butera writes incredible poems."

Ann Christine Tabaka, multi-award-winning poet

"The sheer talent and skill of Philip Butera as a writer simply cannot be disputed. He is a language wizard when using the written word to present imagery, ideas, and feelings that are profound yet easily absorbed by the reader. Additionally, if poetry is meant to be read aloud, Butera's work is satisfying indeed."

Salvatore Alessi, Adjunct Professor of Literature, Canisius College

"I think this is a great book of poetry, a significant accomplishment. It is important that people read what Philip has created."

Michael Griffin, English Professor at Okanagan University College (retired)

"Philip Butera uses words and phrases like an accomplished artist uses color and light. Excellent balance of imagery and abstraction. His command of language is broad and lush."

Nicole Washburn, Editor, and Ghostwriter

"With raw passion and profound psychological perception, Philip's poetry pierces your innermost being."

Eva E. A. Skoe, Ph.D. Professor Emeritus of Psychology

"Philip's beautifully dangerous poetry captivates the reader with intensely revealing intimacy."

Teresa Ann Frazee, Artist, and Poet, Founder of the Boca Museum of Art, Art & Literature Series

From the Author

"I love words.

A word is a thought pared to its most elemental instance.

Now combine words, and you have secrets uncovered,
emotions expressed,

and every moment examined."

From "The Apparition"

Writers are adventurers, explorers, and searchers always looking for the perfect word. I know I do. I need to find that word that conveys precisely what may be hazily circling in my mind. I know the word I think I want but is that word the exact word needed? Is my definition and the dictionary's definition identical? Can I use a particular word and let the phrase "poetic justice" cover any length I need to stretch to make my intended meaning fit?

So many questions. But writers and poets have tools. I have a small hardcover book that I can never remember not having. For more than seventy years, this book has traveled with me, *18,000 Words often Mispronounced*, published at the start of the twentieth century.

I have used it to help me pronounce words. Recently, I became intrigued with the diacritical marks (those dots, lines, and swoops that appear above, below, and occasionally even beside certain letters in words in the book.) Those markings help articulate correctly, and I must admit I love the word- diacritical. It sounds important.

After finding the word and pronouncing it correctly, one must know the true meaning of the word. This is where my classic *Synonym Finder* comes in handy. Sadly, I have been known to get lost in this book filled with words, words, and more words, and, what a bonus, their synonyms. It is like eating delicious Swiss chocolate and extra creamy vanilla ice cream at the same time.

This research will usually lead me to *Dictionary of Problem, Slang, and Unconventional Words* or *Dictionary of Problem Words and Expressions* or *The Describer's Dictionary*, where writers have known to be lost for weeks. Now we have added Funfetti cake and caramel brownies. I may dig further, using a *Dictionary of Misunderstood or Misused Words.* Words, don't you love them? Now, you have the perfect word. But, you do want to know its origin? Then, Voilà (grave accent over the a) the *Oxford Dictionary of English Etymology* comes off the shelf. Or the ever-present *Dictionary of Word Origins* is opened, and once delved into the chocolate eclairs, and chocolate milk is needed to stave off starvation. This journey is never direct nor short. The

book is extensive. What if the word is a verb? This leads us to infinitives, participles, gerunds, and irregular verbs.

If this process began early in the day, it is now close to nightfall. Oh, we can't overlook sentence structure—subjects and predicates, phrases, clauses, pauses, not to forget transformations, punctuation, and words that rhyme. So, reach for the Cheerios, adding both banana and peach topped with blueberries.

There are so many words and so many distracting extraneous things to do. But I am fortunate I have a fellow word lover— close friend, collaborator, editor, educator, writer, and poet. We can talk for hours about diphthongs, dangling modifiers, and on occasion, palindromes and gerunds. Our phone calls are never measured by time because probing questions about words is like extending endlessly after infinite.

I am proud to have her work and mine together in this book. Her imagery, narrative, and expressive daring are outstanding. In poems like *Ruptured Canopies, I am a Consummate Gardener,* and *A Rush of Emotions and Nakedness,* her journey is a vivid invitation for all to step into her emotional realm.

With admiration and respect

I dedicate this book to

Lorna Thomson

Philip Butera

Table of Contents

Philip Butera

Philip Butera

Falls from Grace, Favor and High Places

Under Whitest Mist

Those are not clouds.

Those are stepping stones.

I use them to skip over the moon

and watch speeding comets.

Soaring birds weave a path

through the lightness

past illusions

begun fantasies ago.

As dreams shrug away the night

to come alive,

images capture the invisible

and candor fills the sky.

1

I see you

under whitest mist,

the lyrical

expression of what I desire.

If art is imagination,

you widen the palette

of clarity and distinction

intensifying the heavens.

I am a poet

you are a romantic.

We are a visual ribbon

playing with stars.

You Walked Through Me

You,

walked through me into the night.

A lonely chill remains.

As I look from the bedroom window

to the lake,

the moonlight encourages the frogs to croak deeply

and the ducks to squabble more.

I realize,

humans live by alarm.

Without

precision nor intelligence,

just clanging,

a raucous

of self-doubt and confusion.

A gentle breeze moves the silky yellow curtains

you bought to match the yellow comforter.

You said,

"Dreams in yellow bring harmony."

Philip Butera

But, we were never harmonious.

Me, bound in chaos

and you,

smiling, as if time were your possession,

something between

connivance and crisis.

My heart races as the transition begins,

from vulnerable to loathsome,

anticipating the restlessness

and the aching appeal of alcohol

tinged delusions.

The white Shih-Tzu I bought for you

but was never yours,

wandered in when he heard the door slam.

He pawed my leg,

and his black eyes assured me

he was weary of watching us

pretend

we actually cared.

There was a War Going on Back Then; it Seems There is Always a War Defending Some Gnarled Thicket of Words

I'm sorry,

how could I have forgotten?

But it was so long ago.

We lived in a moody time back then,

tumbling from rebellious late teens into

shoulder-shrugging pretenders.

It hits fast and hard,

learning the world deplores intelligence

and loves those who quietly line up to die,

be it literally or figuratively.

There was a war going on back then,

it seems there is always a war

defending some gnarled thicket of words.

She had long red hair

and eyes that were sometimes green, sometimes blue

but never at ease.

As we lie naked in a small metal bed in a summer
cottage,

she told me stories about Trude Heller's in Greenwich
Village

and having strawberry soup

at the Rainbow Room atop Radio City Music Hall.

With impatient desires,

wish-fulfillment never gains traction,

it just lingers in a latent state.

We never danced; we just created views for ourselves
that would never materialize.

I remember dissecting Holden Caulfield,

she holding a whimsical opinion,

while I, forever curious,

asked about subplots and meanings without implications.

We had intimate moments,

but they seemed more like capturing

an essence of what was emerging,

something to hold the moments together,

more pleasure than passion.

We were mere blossoms, mingling our spirits

as the waves from Lake Erie reached the Canadian
shoreline.

The summer hurried, the moon went through its cycles,
and the stars shined bright.

With Autumn came the scents of cinnamon, pumpkin,
and damp leaves burning.

The amusement park closed, and the houses along the
water's edge were boarded up.

Her hand slipped from mine.

I went to college,

then out to sea wearing a uniform

while

she traveled west

believing in herself and marketing fashion.

Sometime between then and now

with another, then another war in the background,

I received postcards from Italy and France,

she gushed about

so many museums and churches to visit.

I had moved south

discovering living is just an impression of life

and dreams,

fragile memories

yet to be forgotten.

Unphased by masks, time scampered

without looking back,

we would meet occasionally.

War was now part of our vocabulary and barely noticed.

I had become skeptical, and she had become distrustful.

We discussed lies woven in truths and ambitious
adventures

that would never take place.

Soon,

the conversation spun its way

to those days,

those sunshine days.

A reminiscent summer warmth

would

hold us for a few fleeting seconds.

At the funeral service

of a friend whose wounds never scarred

from a long-ago war

that is still slyly defended

I expected to find her,

but

in a world where boots leave deep impressions

she had retreated into herself.

Though we may never

toast the past again

I am grateful

for that summer

of textured epiphanies

where

we had become

part of each other.

The Expanse of Pondering

Not the strict imagination of recapturing

nature but the expanse of pondering what

nature *is,*

that is what intrigues me.

The visual complexity,

not as an entity but as a thought.

A thought appreciative of itself

and seeking expression.

Take hold of the reservoir

toss away the conspiracy,

peel away the rind

and wonder

at the fruit of color, light, and sensuality.

Trade what is familiar

for what is gushingly exceptional.

Push Atlas aside

and invite Euphrosyne

to dance.

My life is measured in falls,

from grace, favor, and high places.

I became a criminal,

normally

a privilege of the wealthy.

I never hitched a ride on a freight train

but I bought a ticket in Toronto

and rode out west,

way out west to the Pacific.

I went the distance

from an idea

I had planned

with my

Cousin.

He headed to SF,

to become an artist

and

I was freewheeling

like Dylan.

It was easier than time traveling

from Naples

to Sicily

like

Caravaggio.
We were the wild, wild horses
English artist Stubbs
should have painted.

Breathe life into the world,

think.

Contemplate,

embrace the figure within the marble.

Stretch a canvas,

sense the mastery of Titian's colors,

awe at his inventiveness,

then dream,

the dream you are complimenting in blues

with oranges

and expand reds into browns

for a scene

of young girls in sumptuous robes

glancing at the

spectacle

of chariots racing.

I opened my mind to psychology

and the martyrs
who once enjoyed my company
took seats away from the bar.
Studying neurology,
introspecting on apples,
checking out books on biochemistry,
playing pinball
and impressing
young women.
The pubs were caves,
where Plato dismissed
the myths
as I bought
rounds of
draft beer.

Stand on Burnaby mountain,
watch the crack in the earth,
being filled by Holst's planets.
Please pay special attention to
the Bringers of Jollity
and the Mystic,

they allow you to confront yourself.

Pull up a mirror; ask yourself,

is it ever too late to marry art

and knowledge into a lifestyle?

Sing Cohen's "Anthem"

loud enough for others to hear,

strip away all the mundane

for the phantasmagorical

and have a propensity for deviance.

Be the one to tell Dante;

maybe he shouldn't be *that* cruel

to the followers of Bacchus

after all, there is no salvation

outside of knowing what you knew.

The wound was still open

in Southeast Asia

justice was the noun, justify the verb

and

young men were the currency.

No verbal opposition

can compete with

numbers and symbols

across a TV screen
leveraging profitable ways
to slip casualties quietly into
an unpowdered body bag.

The Flemish Baroque Nudes by Rubens
make us forgive when we want to blame.
While Boucher's naked Rococo temptresses invite
even the least competent voyeur to enjoy their beauty.
Those resting between Sand and Flaubert realize
what could be a crime in one culture
might be a virtue in another.
And if the underbelly is needed, select Goya's graphic
etchings and let them lead you deep into
history's hypocrisy.

As every truth starts as a fantasy,
and gamblers have a habit of losing time,
the word,
art has a mythical feel
and when all the inquisitorial stains
are removed,
art itself becomes

the most exposed.

We believe what we are told to believe

unless we read

the Existentialists

who

remembered the future

and recognized

the false and the genuine.

They appreciated

that

art, like the depth

of what cannot be known,

is boundless.

Being breezy, idealistic

and brash

I ordered two rounds of drinks

to impress

a fair woman with thin lips

wearing a short red skirt.

She was

sexy and intelligent,

Philip Butera

knew the value of words.

and

how to use them.

When I asked, "If images capture the invisible,"

she quipped,

"If so, render yourself defenseless."

The Stunning Echoing Silence after the Stampeding of a Thousand Stallions

A friend told me she was lonely.

I asked, "What does that feel like?"

"The stunning, echoing silence

after the stampeding

of a thousand

stallions."

I ventured from one Poe poem to another,

into a misty realm,

awakening awareness with insight.

My mind, not a realistic component of the now,

was entirely sure a storm was mounting,

pending my way.

Those spirited horses still raged,

unhindered by blind spots in front and behind.

They galloped to the heavens,

bypassing

the brambles of certainty.

Soon,

I was moving from one color to another

in "The Masque of the Red Death."

The differences in brightness and shadow overcame me.

I stiffened in the vermillion room

as those magnificent horses faded.

The sky was ebony black,

it felt like the darkness came

from somewhere other than the night.

Cold arctic eyes, large and chilling, found me.

They expected me to be grateful.

But I did not know how to feel,

and without any anticipation,

my reflection became a shimmering mist

from a decaying mosaic.

The room swelled with rolling waves.

One beautiful horse,

mottled cinnamon with charcoal mane

and a golden spray of stars on his muzzle,

Philip Butera

came back for me,

but I could not mount.

I was heavy from wetness.

I remained at a distance,

spiraling from where imagination had little fear

into the tragic fall of the damned.

Sleep never woke me.

The icy arctic eyes flowed into a body,

a voluptuous woman now,

glowing white, beguiling with long slender arms.

She took control of the horse.

The room spun, and the seams

where aloneness collected was scarred.

I fell in love with the woman,

for I was all colors deadening,

and she was guilt fleeing.

Interrupted by emotions,

images and ideas disappeared,

leaving an uncomfortable undertone.

Like the distance,

memories are chased but never caught.

My friend fled the strange for the familiar,

praying that loneliness

would not tumble into fear.

> *In the minds of characters,*
>
> *I create,*
>
> *"The Raven" reigns supreme,*
>
> *but I am confined between the words,*
>
> *knotted in the complexity*
>
> *of bewilderment.*

Nightmares no Longer Framed by Sleep

It is me

I can't quite

comprehend.

With every breath,

vipers stir.

Tragedies take

center stage

and shadows

reveal

impending misfortunes.

One thought

corrupts the next.

The flames, torrents,

storms

prevail

and still

time gilds memories.

I sit in my study

reading Paradise Lost,

a smirk on my face,

disbelieving the many shelves

could ever collapse

with every book opening

to the proper page

to that paragraph

that defines misfortune.

Where Bovary, Gatsby,

and Hamlet

see no shallowness

being themselves.

The books become extensions of dreams.

They become me playing host

to

those who will always

be in places too high to approach.

In a dark room, there are two intersecting shafts of
shimmering light.

I am a gambler,

across from me is the face of my own ghost.

Philip Butera

It is the last hand,

and the

pot is overflowing.

The first card dealt me is an eight,

two more show up.

I am confident

but

D'Artagnan has three ladies

and Cinderella in a low-cut, gold cocktail dress

smiles winningly

and

reveals

all kings

but

Stella, by Starlight, is wild.

I come to think,

what if what remains

is unmoved

though swept away?

In a room,

24

where imagination

fills in the gap

between

intuition and thought

I remain possessed

by nightmares

no longer framed by sleep.

While I was away, the Room Seduced Her

The Impressionists created a new language

when they put their brushes on the canvas.

Wagner revolutionized opera, and Debussy quieted

theatres with his delicate compositions.

D. H. Lawrence reinvented the romantic novel.

Rodin established modern sculpture.

I need to know these particulars,

I need to know art,

that is how I understand myself.

My study was once an unused bedroom.

Neither child nor guest ever laid their head

on the soft arm of the old leather sofa.

I occasionally do- I close my eyes

and reflect on my passions.

I see undefined images,

I hear voices that fall through my thoughts.

The wind enters from the opened window

and brings the smells of the season,

they travel the house,

exiting out the dining area's glass doors

into the screened patio.

They carry on through the garden

and continue to the lake

where the ducks and birds float beneath clouds.

There are books in this room,

many books,

so many kinds of books;

fiction, non-fiction, poetry, and plays.

Above them, all are hardcover books

on art, artists, and authors.

They remain on shelves, on chairs, on desks,

in boxes, on the floor, and in the closet.

There are CDs in this room, hundreds of them

mainly classical, also jazz, and the American songbook.

The walls are full of paintings, full of color.

It is my yearning for meaning

in an absurd world.

I think Camus or Buddha said that,

and I, at a young age,

agreed.

We all know life is a gallop toward death,

a prizefight, against time,

with a brief discussion in between

about either *how much* or *how come.*

I have an enthusiasm for art.

It is the high wire, a disorder of imagination,

that never entirely reveals itself,

though it feigns a logic and reason

within its dialogue of reality.

We are either the executioners

or the coils

that wrap around them.

But artists are neither.

They are an evolving exclamation,

a dysfunctional blurring of mind and emotion.

I have had lovers tell me

this room is the personification of what I desire to be,

a certainty- within the chaos, yet an anarchist,

even the cunning Odysseus would appreciate.

One who levitates truth

to the highest level while poignantly,

and creatively addressing what the soul ponders.

One woman said

while I was away, the room seduced her,

every move I made to pleasure her,

the room imitated.

Everything I ever whispered to her was made sweeter

from being in this room,

glowing with the smooth richness of integrity,

that wisdom epitomizes.

A close friend that likes to share a beer with me,

never fully enters this room.

He says it makes him feel uncomfortable.

He dismisses the books.

To him, each one is a casket

waiting to be hauled away by contemporary pallbearers.

He believes I have sacrificed the authenticity of living

for dreams dreamt at the edge of futility.

My dog likes my study.

Maxx sits on a bench

and watches what transpires outside.

He barks at large trucks

and any vehicle that pulls into our driveway.

His round dark eyes

follow those on bikes and skateboards,

women who pass wearing earphones,

and men speaking too loudly.

Sometimes,

he just lies on the soft fabric,

warmed by the sun,

his eyes close

and a thousand

adventures begin.

Irises in the foreground, and Almond Blossoms Before me

A Mediterranean afternoon,

warm with moisture in the air.

Irises in the foreground and almond blossoms before me.

A stunning woman in all white,

with long white hair wearing white-framed sunglasses,

looks up to the disappearing rainbow.

> *I stumble over who I have become,*
>
> *a fictional persona of who I should be,*
>
> *at my best*
>
> *when I am someone else.*

The woman smiles at me, a friendly, hello smile,

a smile that dresses me into the role I play best.

In the distance, oak, beech, and elm trees

provide shade for those unaware of us.

There is a sea full of sirens,

singing sweetly.

The stunning woman seems to be waiting.

Slowly moving clouds

become images against a turquoise sky.

> *I excel in the confessional approach*
>
> *to meet beautiful ladies.*
>
> *A certainty I created,*
>
> *not discovered.*
>
> *Joy entwines about fear,*
>
> *while*
>
> *countenance, and coolness*
>
> *avow my interest.*

A tall, handsome man with dark wavy hair,

fashionably dressed in shades of browns,

signals and begins to advance toward her.

Towards the us,

I have created.

My dog's insistence breaks my reverie.

We move toward the adjacent hedged garden,

maybe, the woman will follow.

> *I know there are images of the eye*
>
> *and images of the mind.*
>
> *I understand language and reason,*

light, and shadow.

I know I am

between a life

and a belief in living.

White and brown go together,

but words clash and collide

when they are mere amusements,

the brain uses to un-comprehend the world.

In my room,

as yellow as Van Gogh painted for Gauguin,

there are books from floor to ceiling.

I hate them.

I love them.

I feel my ghost in them,

restless and brooding, curious and frightened.

On the walls,

there are hundreds of paintings.

I hear them, and I see beneath the hues

they are dreams of others

now aloft in my thoughts.

I am elsewhere, elsewhere from wherever I am.

My thoughts

churn in realms where phrases

can never express

what paintings have revealed.

From the narrow window above the vase of sunflowers,

I watch the wind address the day.

I am always on the eve of splendor,

moments from misfortune.

I see you,

I touch you, and I envy you.

Nothing interferes with your motion.

You are not stitched together like me.

You are whole, complete with confidence and courage.

A stunning woman all in white, with long white hair

wearing white-framed sunglasses.

I look up the word,

sorrow,

sadness is there, but not sad.

Is there a difference between sadness and sad?

Is one a condition,

the other what I feel

when I see pity in your eyes?

You know you are the stunning woman in all white,

with long white hair wearing white-framed sunglasses.

You are the distance I can never reach.

I see no defense for myself.

In the far corner of a fractured vastness

I uncloak the night,

hoping my bareness will be a beacon

out of the dark,

but I find I am the darkness.

No embrace will ever rise me

from the unraveling

at the edges of recognition.

I will always be the one

stunning woman all in white, with long white hair,

wearing white-framed sunglasses

must leave behind.

I am a Voyeur on a Palate of Frenzied Hues

In a dream,

there is only distance-

impressionistic and inviting.

Trees weep against restless clouds,

rushing waves crash into a broken wall

and it begins to crumble.

The swells create echoes and shadows

I struggle to comprehend.

Within this dream,

I am

no longer performing

as me

or myself

I am layers of sad grays on a black canvas

without form or discipline,

just an ill-defined

appearance.

All are flawed,

except

for you.

You are dreamlike,

even in a dream.

A delicate crimson apparition

amidst swirling cobalt blues

and trailed by wispy nebulous yellows.

You are Athena

appearing as Aphrodite.

An awakening horizon

that appears and reappears,

becoming

what is sought,

but never captured.

In this dream,

we are about

to touch.

In lush greens and sensual violets,

your breasts are bare

for my kisses

but around me,

cold gusts from nightmares

long veiled,

whirl

separating us.

Lost in this dream,

I run to my mother,

whose arms cannot quite reach me,

while my father

navigates the oceans

in his dreams

looking for escape routes

to free himself.

My tears accumulate.

I am there, and there,

and nowhere.

And nowhere

is a marshmallowy quicksand

of refusals and barriers

buried

within myself.

Through the

cascading abstraction

of entry places

too dark to enter,

the silky mist from an angel's wings

opens my eyes

and sharpens my vision.

Now, I recognize

who I am.

A voyeur

on a palate of frenzied hues

searching

for a book of poems

never written,

listening

to a sonata never played.

The dreamscape

slowly fades,

a reflection in a gilded mirror

comes into view.

I am alone,

no longer restless,

all the words, scores, and colors

are

echoes and shadows,

dissolving

in memories of silvery light.

Unmoved by Storms

The distance swells with rolling waves,

sweet destructive forces

colliding and caressing

without shadow or boredom.

Angry deep blue swells

rush to jagged cliffs.

Forward motion halts

and

strength dissipates.

Power and beauty,

unbound by reason or consequence

defines

the sensuality of being.

Color and light gathers within us,

and the eloquence of emotional experience,

becomes a reality

for dreamers and dreamcatchers.

My daughter,

unmoved by storms

sees words in the wind

and with her hands

she paints the world

in rhapsodic indulgences.

She separates time from eternity.

Her green eyes hold imagination

before illusion.

She picks up her baton

and the orchestra

of sky, water, and gusts

becomes

a bright and enlightening

kaleidoscope

of wonder and enchantment

that lasts a lifetime

of forevers.

The Slurry of Consequences

I remember when I was young,

my uncle saying,

while I watched a football game,

"It's all fixed."

I didn't want to believe him,

yet in my heart, a hard stone was placed.

I grew and went away to college.

And whenever I watched a sporting event,

my uncle's words came to mind,

and the stone grew.

Philosophy interested me, so I read about wisdom.

I read about truth.

I read about ethics and morals.

I learned the difference between

Mythology and Psychology.

I thought about thinking.

Art interested me,

so I read about gifted artists.

Words interested me,

so I read the great authors.

Reading interested me,

so I read more and more,

from comedy to poetry.

I traveled.

When I stepped from the scholarly

into the slurry of consequences

called the real world,

the gravity of my uncle's words took hold.

The stone was maturing into a crystal

with razor-sharp edges.

I observed nature,

and I observed behavior.

When the oracles told us

that the stars no longer wanted human sacrifice,

the cunning merchants

positioned themselves

as God's direct interpreters.

Malleable horizons became disclosures

discussed in whispered tones

with those in the know.

Those in the know

were those who disoriented

the space

between ordinary and undetermined.

Human sacrifice survived

under a sweeter name

and became the spectator sport

of those having more and more.

And wanting more.

Words gave me insight.

I knew the killing storm,

the shameful had brewed, was fictitious.

And when I was detained

and asked of what worth am I.

I knew my uncle's remark was true,

"It's all fixed."

We all Sink into the Swill

I seem to be swimming in thoughts

that may not be mine.

I know that is mad,

but not any more insane than

loving in vain,

containing a tsunami,

or escaping the labyrinth.

At times we all sink into the swill.

Those thoughts that gather at the back of our mind,

the ones that are not polite.

The ones loosely chained

to angels,

we no longer trust.

Books, paintings, and music surround me.

Literature never expects you to be grateful.

Art assumes your trepidation is minimal,

and sound replaces one pain with another.

Mix them,

run them through a funnel,

then a sifter,

purify the results.

Then look into a mirror

and have a conversation with

your other-self,

the hidden one with the forbidden desires.

The devious one,

armed with claws that flash when threatened.

I pace catwalks, reflecting on philosophy,

ignoring any glazed views of pastoral landscapes.

I love the brutal thrashing of actual thoughts.

But sometimes

the novocaine of being,

cannot reach

the most profound places

we must descend.

Consciousness is a navigational tool,

an optic that layers modern thought

with hypocritical realism

and as

language becomes bondage,

you discover

the mask of arrogance

is a treaty with yourself.

Subject and object

meld

and an abyss is created.

> As if dancing
>
> and losing my way
>
> I fall off the mountain
>
> through the thickets
>
> of classical literature
>
> and
>
> irrational history
>
> into realms and reams
>
> of the mind's abstract intelligibility.

The plummet

is an untangling of

observation and introspection.

The fall

strips away the conventional,

the accepted,

and what emerges

is the devious,

the cunning me,

the one without an image.

Through a series of twisted

allegories and spiritual performance pieces

untwisting,

my intellectual curiosity

breathes freely.

I comprehend the climax is not the landing,

but

the absolute nakedness

once the fall is complete.

There are times

when I want

to inhabit

Dorian Gray's liberties.

To have the flair of a psychopath.

Philip Butera

Their blamelessness.

No social shrewdness shades their hostility,

they are a sticky slime

bound

to the underside of virtue.

I never trust the truth,

unless I,

all of them that I am

are beneath the bluest of skies,

far from ordinations,

clear of flocks

chased by antagonists,

and resolute

within the magic of knowing

we all work our way out

of dreadful dreams.

My thought designs become cavalier

freed by metaphysical verse.

Frame of mind disappears

and

bleak midwinter

becomes

juvenile spring.

Then,

somewhere between Virgil and Nietzsche

I ponder the black miracles

and

empty the dictionary of its words.

Remembering that inspiration

has limitations

bound to intelligence.

I whirl through the abridgments

of beauty and passion

understanding

that wisdom's birth is not divine

but a lyricism

wrapped

free of false constraints.

Naked on every stage

aware that genius

is much

more than creativity.

I am urged

by all those

indulgent nudes in master paintings,

to join

Jefferson, Marat, and Shelly.

I have learned,

defiance is the authorship

of influence.

With operatic drama

I proclaim,

I am singular

and I have the strength,

the knowledge

and the right

to start

a revolution.

I Gamble with Priests (II)

Across the harbor, at a tavern,

red and blue neon lights are visible.

I gamble with priests there,

they take my money and bless my soul.

The priests say I am vulnerable

because there are no prayers for what I want.

My collie and I study art together.

I read Poe, and he examines statues.

We travel up and down the line, sometimes we cross it.

When priests tell me luck is God's gift,

I ask about the martyrs.

As they dwell upon redemption,

I smile,

knowing

I am comfortable

being who I am.

Sometimes as I drink beer and write poetry,

my dog courts a liver and white spaniel.

The spaniel is owned by a tall lady with short yellow
hair

who sings at the church.

While our dogs amuse each other,

we watch seagulls play above the waves.

The lady's cottage and breath smell like cinnamon tea,

her breasts and legs smell like sesame oil.

She told me she once painted cabins,

in harvest fields against snow-capped mountains.

She always seemed to be available

when God was nowhere to be found.

The lady took our dogs to live with her

in a small beach town in Ontario.

She promised to send photos of their puppies.

I miss laying in her little bed under the white sheets,

dried by the sea breezes.

I miss the anticipation of being with her,

the surprise of her words

and the openness

of her ideas.

Priests still visit the bar where I drink.

They still ask more of me than I can give.

We discuss profound discoveries,

and we gamble.

When I get home, a black cat cannot be seen.

Dogs greet you,

but cats are skeptical.

They creep about, sure-footed and silent,

never trusting what they are questioning.

I call the black cat "Chance"

since her green eyes reveal

she is determining

whether or not to give me away.

Philip Butera

Punishing me for Promises, you made about me
to Yourself

You lied,

and I misunderstood.

I wait for your return,

one hour, two,

how many?

You want me to be someone else,

starry-eyed from forbidden dreams,

not a tale of my telling.

Your taillights disappeared,

and I dammed myself

for

being unable to package heaven

and present it to you.

The voices in my head

curse their claustrophobic lives

being captive in my mind.

I pace,

and find me at the window.

As a child,

I would stare out the window

and watch the snowfall,

waiting for my father.

He always forgot he made me a promise

to come home instead of going to a tavern.

Time would pass,

anxiety would grow, I would feel hollow

while I made up stories to myself

that he would not come home drunk

and argue with my mother.

Memories and sorrow,

sometimes the black glossy tape

intended to bind live wires

needs to be used

once more.

The old bindings are crusted, torn, and come away easily

as I have aged.

The tugging and pulling has made my

heart less amenable to

mending.

No matter, the tape is unending

but I am frightened

these wounds will never scar

and someday,

nuts and bolts will be needed.

The clumsiness of anticipation gnaws at me.

It does not count the time; it analyses every moment,

all the while

offering alternatives to foolishness,

which lingers,

pretending to know

what the soul craves.

Those feelings of inadequacy have never left me,

when one minute becomes the next,

then the next,

I am that damp eyed child again,

watching the snow pile,

higher and higher,

and though it is beautiful

it is unsettling.

Now, you have run away,

punishing me for promises

you made about me

to yourself.

I am incapable of understanding

why we quarrel when we should be celebrating.

As I punish myself for my insecurities,

you arrive home,

drunk and unhappy,

swearing that destiny has abandoned you.

Our voices become deadly swords that pierce and slice,

we are my parents.

You pour vodka into a Waterford glass,

then close the bedroom door.

I gravitate to the window,

it is night

without moon, stars

Philip Butera

or expectations.

There is no snow,

yet I watch snow pile up

higher

and ever higher.

On a Backroad Where Medea told
Jason not to be Afraid

It's the end; we are two faces on blank pages sharing our last toast.

Gleaming angels bet

on my

curdling in loneliness,

while fallen angels

measure

blame against reason.

Cold but dazzling

without regrets,

dismissive of recollections,

you are instantly released

from any suspension

between pain and hell.

On a backroad

where Medea told Jason not to be afraid,

and the new-self remembers the old,

with a sarcastic smile,

and a witty retort to my refection

I drink to time unraveling.

Dice roll, wheels spin,

and I see images in words,

words in paintings

while

you dismiss dreams

and calculate the opportunity.

On separate mountains,

we look deep into the night to see what the sun offers.

Another grand theatre performance

alight by sweet sensuality but lacking inventiveness

and darkly framed in degrading

decrescendos.

I believe life

is meant to imitate art,

unlocking hidden meanings in temptation;

maidens with beautiful breasts, Christ on the cross,

lovers in pastoral settings,

ships in a storm,

and wistfulness bursting through imagination.

In your life, there are no

snow globes to be shaken,

you can lose, but you always win.

I never trade places with my shadow

like those dulled,

mistaking faith for maturity.

I prefer possibilities over a definite

and

when the Oracle of Delphi

temps me with contentment,

I always smile, snapping my fingers,

to the *Summer Wind*.

I ignore mirrors

and shards of glass

as I

grin at the ladies,

raise the bet,

and gauge the difference

between discretion and deception.

Philip Butera

On weekends you play heavenly hostess

at your lover's summer villa.

While architects and politicians

admire garden sculptures and Depression-era photos

by Dorothea Lange

insatiable corporate executioners

descend

from a trojan horse.

        Ignoring the obvious

        my guardian angel and I

        skip from star to star,

        occasionally

        we fall through the clouds

        narrowly landing

        on comets

        that have brightened

        to catch us.

No Longer a Crusader for Antiquity's Heaven

I am

mad from thinking,

mad from loving,

mad from being.

Disenchanted with illusions

and

tired of expectations.

I pace

within my mind,

aware of the

encircling darkness.

One dream disrupts another.

Images become

thinning ellipses.

tempering

the language of awakening.

Desire and sorrow

spill

from reveries

into

ghostly imperfections

un-coloring

how time

passes.

No longer a crusader

for antiquity's heaven.

I cling to me,

a lonely melody,

in spiraling descent

distracted

only

by a poet's

romance with madness.

Philip Butera

You Catch the Stars
"Love is just a lie made to make you blue"*

*Love Hurts lyrics by Boudleaux Bryant © BMG Rights Management, House Of
Bryant Publications

In the cold winter moonlight,

I shout your name to the wind.

After calls and falls,

wheels travel a thousand miles,

and nothing seems to change.

You catch the stars,

 I lose them in the clouds.

A dull sense surrounds the emptiness

and it never seems to pass.

My illusions are no match for your clarity,

yet the landscapes of our souls

are spilled from ultramarine and expectation.

We should have lingered,

immersed in that lush space

where dreams and imagination caught us undressing

Philip Butera

and the sublime deep sound of a cello

evaporated the blame

neither

of us could forgive.

Paradise is Only a Mystery if You Have no Life to Exploit

I made up my history,

while you were dancing around the moon,

I crept upon a star and carefully crafted the

the sentiment of why I am appealing.

Differing lives are lived between each moment,

one filled with a quick wit and fallen distances

and the other uphill, with hardened scars.

On the high wire,

where restrained enthusiasm escalates

you discover,

heaven has a cover charge.

But the gloom plummets substantially,

as you realize, paradise is only a mystery

if you have no life to exploit.

My passions shun daydreams,

I enjoy the loneliness of night.

Rainbows also appear in dreams,

follow the arc to your signature

open the invitation, discard the warning

scamper head-long past

the superficial draped pleasantries

to where darkness and imagination

become the beginnings

of delightful bewilderment.

Never,

trust a mirror.

Smash it,

be attentive

to the brush in your thoughts

and the canvas in your mind.

I overhear you say something about natural wildness.

Your blouse is silvery, your skin tanned, and

you have everyone's attention.

But I have yours.

You give the room sparkle, and I provide character.

With guiltless audacity,

you approach and ask if I am free.

Those around us fade to the periphery

and catch a glimpse of passion unraveling.

I illuminate my poetic path,

implying

you are the one I am meant to impress.

We waste little time; we use language

to break the bondage,

unveiling the tears, we have wept

to create the voice

needed to bathe

each other in pure delight.

Many different spheres attempt to accomplish

what an ellipse does naturally.

You and I are two fixed points

added to the same constant.

Without possessing,

we become color and shape

and our hearts dazzle with a profound capacity

to reveal what time has eliminated

from our expectations.

With all the splendors of misfortune,

we venture into the shadows,

where

the certainty of becoming anonymous

coalesces with celestial light.

And even when resting together

garbed in the intoxicating quest for pleasure,

listening to a Brahms violin concerto,

there is one uncertain,

curious inconsistency,

in every Eden,

there is a serpent.

After desiring you,

I watched Icarus,

fly too close to the sun.

You were captivated

by Prometheus when he stole fire back from Zeus

and presented an eternal flame to you.

In flurries of spectacle and celebration

Bacchus is at your side.

Your dalliances possess

the singular richness of being lively,

yet your spirit remains unsettled.

I have been called smooth,

I have been called insolent.

When I was on Everest with damsels in red,

I was tasked to whittle away the boredom,

so arm in arm,

we lept

and fell among the many names used to describe

the movement of the soul.

Now, with apparitions of seasons past,

I watch angry waves

crash against the jagged rocks.

The darkness enlightens me.

Water is fluid.

Water vapor surrounds.

And when water freezes,

the molecules move farther apart.

As I become wetter,

I am reminded about the indifference of being.

I made up my history,

I am neither here nor there,

neither mad nor sane.

Just a thought, I am thinking

on my way from poet

to virtuoso.

Sphinx of Another Fall

Prelude

At the bar, she sips an aperitif.

She is,

the elegant reward after a dangerous crossing,

well worth the risk.

Tall, with long blonde hair,

in a black dress.

When our eyes meet,

an inkling of winter

shivers through me.

Under blue-green lights,

we become acquainted.

She is a cool breeze

moving through a moonless night.

I am a peacock,

emerging from a paint box,

a twinkling without anchor.

In my bedroom

as I watch her undress,

there are echoes from a prior crime,

where the victim was found guilty

though the jury

never heard the case.

Interlude

Whether in heaviness or emptiness

the bell tolls.

Time becomes a responsibility,

and even before,

I say something,

she makes it seem wrong.

There are no corners, in what remains,

only sharp edges.

I am obsolete;

a stem whose flower has dried.

Dawn breaks.

A tempest finds its path.

One voice speaks over another,

deepening wounds.

All that is reasonable,

is no longer valid.

We've become the locked door

keeping the other out.

Postlude

Somewhere she occupies herself

with matters of fencing.

The effectiveness of distance,

is being absent when rainclouds appear.

I cling to illusions, as I dream away,

stumbling again,

a sphinx

of

another fall.

Fragments of Long-Lost Conversations

Introduction

Though I may be from my past,

      I am the most recent me.

   Brooding and restless,

      seeing

         the future as

            a corridor of strange cries.

    With every breath I take, serpents stir.

    Knitting needles take the place of ideas.

    They create evolving constellations.

    There is a central vision, then a scream,

      devolving into a bloody uprising.

    Tragedies occur, and I search the debris.

My mind dwells on fragments of long-lost conversations.

One thought alters the next; thinking becomes puzzling.

Whips smack the flesh; self-discovery is never painless.

Blurred by tears,

I remain possessed

by nightmares spilling from blurred daydreams.

I swirl in self-expression,

keeping the doubters and their influences at a distance.

The claws of transformation dig deep into my

soul; they search for impressionistic notes

to strike at the exact moment necessary.

The direction changes.

I am swept into a projection of myself.

Alight and entering

with inexplicable swiftness, I appear to meet myself,

and all those identities

that never reflected

to myself,

become pieces of dreams never dreamt.

There,

I am over there, and there, and here.

I am what I have

thought I was,

while thinking

about

the thoughts I have of me.

First Phase

When I find the precise words needed to express what my heart proposes, light emanates from my wounds, and healing begins. Regarding distances, the corridors in mind give way to bastions of masterpieces; those creative statements of clarity and excellence share the sole purpose to evoke what the questionless have suppressed. The accords where Henri Rousseau's Lion innocently roams Van Gogh's Starry Night while Beethoven plays his moonlight sonata, and Gauguin finds a place along with Poe to discard their restlessness.

If only saints have visions, then I have clarity.

Second Phase

The lake is calm; mottled mallard ducks float freely, some in pairs, some have single males following them. Moms lead a small cadre of ducklings around the blue water. I toss them seeds and small berries. Sometimes in the morning, I find a number at my patio door resting on the damp grass. My Shih Tzu is indifferent to them. He neither barks nor chases. He watches from under the gardenia bushes putting up his small black nose to sniff the moist air.

I must give back to the winds, the secrets I can never reveal. Disguises will be needed, and I have chosen to be myself. Scars will lose their stories as brushstrokes exhale the most fragile of colors. The cold will keep me at bay, and the warmth of forgiving myself will joust with the sanity of my futurist thoughts. I can't discern my value. I can conceive dialogues with women I have loved and the devils they chastised after leaving me.

I rest on a white wicker patio chair; I lay comfortably, and the ducks, now relaxed, remain in the shade under palm trees. My dog finds a spot under my chair to keep him from the warming sun.

I live in Florida.

Is live the correct word?

After all, that went before,

crashed

I found myself in Florida,

not that the crashing has subsided.

I gush with anticipation and defy fate's persistence to crowd my conscious efforts to journey within my psyche. I have the key, but grasping reality is as elusive as cracking wisps emanating from a fire fueled by moments in passing.

Two gray squirrels usually appear; they silently climb down a large palm tree, always alert for other animals. Then, cautiously, they dash to the area under the orange hibiscus bushes, where they gather up the assorted nuts I have left for them. Finally, they give each other vocal and bodily signals to communicate.

From somewhere to my right, I hear the television, the news, the endless news, the supposed news shouts at me. Why does it want me to know what they think they know? I am not unread. I am not uneducated, but I am uninterested.

I encounter the unexpected beneath the graves of distinction. As I delve deeper, I become more abstract. It is unexplained, fundamentally different, and my understanding is, in many ways, contrary to the meaning being proposed. I scream I need to escape from the voices who convert slogans into processes and ignorance into gold. They watch me weep when I learn that abundance means slicing precisely at the neck and laughing as the head drops into the trash bin.

I am reading "The Antichrist" again. Nietzsche fascinates me. Authors that make me think interest me, especially philosophers. Though I enjoy good mysteries and well-written poems, I also appreciate writers who love language and apply it like a great painter who uses color and contrast.

I want to shout out to my neighbor to pick up a book; you will never trap reality listening to salespeople on TV, and everyone on TV is selling. Reason must be in touch with objective truth. I love paraphrasing intellectuals while drinking cold beer.

On my own, I bathe in the silence at the end of all phrases concerning human weakness. It is deafening, louder than stillness, more significant than what the present unfolds. While I hunt for something worth believing, thoughts collide with impressions, and impressions overpower sensations. A precipice appears, with a thousand shattered eternities below. The earth shakes, but I balance the corruptness with rhythmic anticipation. I jump and bounce and alter conviction into a force artists can use to hold the extraordinary at length from the logical.

Third Phase

More skittish than the squirrels is Hazel, a rabbit named after the main character in "Watership Down." Hazel has no regular schedule; he comes around every week or so. When I see him, I zip into the house for small carrots and nuts. I place them in the grassy corridor between my home and my neighbor's. There are bushes and greenery for him to hide and hop. Hazel always seems to be on the move, for he never consumes the food I leave out for him. But all the food has disappeared by morning light.

From a pit so foul that nothing can prosper, the persuasion of emotions is explained by definitions of differing moods dissolving. I toss away my masks and let my inner-self come through the tentativeness of diminishment. I comprehend that I am brief. That only I can influence myself. Remoteness becomes the enemy, and hereafter a greeting from candy cane tricksters.

My dog, Maxx, has been called a Zen dog. He rarely barks unless he needs to tell me he would like to venture outside or inside, but I must accompany him. I have never seen him chase another animal. Instead, he makes himself comfortable on the soft grass and searches the land and seascape, his nose leading his head to move from side to side.

The beautiful Egyptian goose, a long way from Africa, decides to roost under a nearby palm tree. She must be a female wanting to get away from the blustering of the males who are usually honking, neck stretching, and displaying their feathers in remarkable ways. These geese have gained respect from the locals because they seem to be at the center when all the bird groups gather.

Large slow-moving poison toads appear, but Maxx pays them no mind. The toads have no significance to him. Eventually, the toads vanish, and Maxx's eyes seem to fix and, like me, ponder. I know he must filter out the droning of the television news. Why is it still called news? It is arrogant entertainment, assuaging the egos of those who chose to be conversant on what they want to hear.

My mind, crushed by the weight of its will to defy shapes within tattered definitions, stampedes from the literal into the symbolic. This gives life to a creative nuance that must nourish itself. Sounds and fragrances define the line of a colorful horizon. There I am, chasing you, my hand grasps your leg, we stumble, and I fall on top of you. Mindlessness becomes nakedness; our eyes savor the destiny we are creating. Being one befits us, not sex but a mysterious orchestration forms, tongues, and fingers find it difficult to linger; they must move, they probe and taste. Satie's Gymnopédies frames our aura, and images we have of ourselves meld as we step from dreams into each other's remembrances.

A year ago, a green iguana appeared. I noticed the animal stayed stationary for long periods, usually claiming a spot several houses down on the bank of the lake. When the iguana did move, he was quick and fleeting. I learned iguanas possess sharp serrated teeth and can grow to over five feet long. They are not attractive creatures. There are three now that call this area home. Two are green, and one is a pale blue-gray. I know they are herbivores but do occasionally eat small animals, so ducklings are in danger. If Maxx were to show his disdain and attack the iguanas for ducks, squirrels, or bunnies on their menu, he could become critically ill.

All that I thought about thinking unlaces and slithers through layers of pure color, pure tones, pure marble, and as I fly like all artists who step beyond madness, I can only express myself by exploiting the language of emotion. When self-hatred jostles ahead, I remove all the non-essentials leaving corners of coherence, isolating all fury that condemnation cannot asphyxiate. Please take my hand. I say to myself if I am myself. Do I recognize me as me? If not, Maxx always does.

I am familiar with the tiny, finger-sized geckos; their colors vary from green to black. I don't mind them at all; they go about their business, darting around for food or mates. They invisibly roam inside the house but can be seen rushing around the patio. They like to hide below things. Sometimes I find a dead gecko next to an inside window. It saddens me. Many things sadden me these days.

The news is irritating, and I wish my neighbor would tame the noise. Why do news people shout? They inaccurately moralize and believe they are on the same plan as preachers—another set of rescuers of few and takers of plenty. How foolish. Anyone with intelligence knows that observation is the highest form of prayer. I am paraphrasing Leonardo Di Vinci, and it is never incorrect to follow his lead.

I understand the turmoil and what "nothing" means now. How smart of you to leave nothing in my holster. Nothing can hold more ammunition than any weapon. Nothing is the goal we should all try to attain. It is no snake; it is what the snake craves after swallowing Brutus and Judas. Nothing is the richness of vulnerability. The flesh revealed is ass, crotch, chest, face, and brains but not the mind because the mind is a meticulous diminishment, a phantom void of conviction, therefore the greatest of all assassins.

I've come to respect birds, Anhinga, Snail Kite, Ibis, Blue Jay, Wood Stork, Grackle, Blue Heron, Egrets, and many appear during the day. The lesser and medium-sized birds recognize that they will be sharing food when they see Maxx, so they sing, tweet, tweet, cheep, chirp, and anxiously anticipate their meal.

Soon, my "flock" surrounds the area between the patio and lake. The Fête Galante begins. The larger birds that fish also find their way to us. They know that I will toss food, crackers, and bread, sometimes pasta, to the ducks in the water. Crumbs drop from the duck's bills; fish gather beneath, waiting to catch fallen morsels. That is when the hunting birds strike and spear the fish swimming at the shoreline. Birds are intelligent animals. I like their sounds and their sense of trust. It is better to watch, listen, and learn from them than stare at ludicrous bobbing heads on television with their unappealing mouths seeking to leave their dropping into your mind.

I wrap myself in barbed wire and align my thoughts with heightening distractions evolving from the monotony of not becoming who I want to be. My ego objects to my accomplishments. And a peculiar apparition that I have concocted has taken possession of my ideas, leaving me to reflect on yesterday's yet to come. I supremely love to orchestrate thinking, it gives substance to the essence of being, and art is what dreamers do. I am a thinker, artist, and dreamer, which means I am always in pain because I cannot always grasp what I fashion.

Titian thought art is color, light, and sensuality. Haydn meant to please. In contrast, Bacon, the artist, wanted to express anguish and futility, so how can I breathe imaginative life into cleverness ribbons and produce literate notions? Beethoven wanted to impress, and I, as an unknown poet, well, I am in suspension between art and life. In other words, I am death desiring meaning for my crime of not being. But I can't scream; I cannot cheer, hence why not a life of single-minded crime? Crime being the reevaluation of the vanishing point of convention, which most artists have openly embraced. So I will hand you the scalpel, carefully cut open my chest and allow access to my heart. Should we expect the Serpent, Eve, or both?

Fourth Phase

There used to be another white wicker chair. She used to sit there, mainly in the early evenings. We had met briefly once at a party, many years before our meeting by coincidence at a party again. One evening as a slivered moon appeared, she said, "You ought to have approached me that night, all those years ago when we were young. I would have left with you. We could have traveled west, and my kids would have been our children. I would have studied art, and you would have gotten your doctorate."

I said, "I wasn't responsible back then and not very trustworthy."

Her face broke into a broad, warm smile as she said, "You would have been both because I would have made you happy."

"Made me happy," no one ever said that to me. Like no other color can be red, I felt fate, faith, and art come together, and all the stains of my life became slight blemishes. A mythical feel centered on me, and an experiential realism consumed me. Optimism became art itself. I ceased to have any disorder of imagination, for it had jelled into redemption.

I read somewhere; every truth starts with a fantasy. Months later, sitting on that same chair at twilight, she told me she had met someone. That they were in the same business, with plenty in common, she handed me her glass, all the vodka gone, and sympathetically said, "I never loved you."

Finally, my absurdity is realized. I am an image of myself disappearing as moments tilt into what can never become. Stained-glass love affairs appear to be light-sensitive and fragile to wind gusts. I am. That is all. The removal of me from myself into words has now become an obsession.

At night, when I take Maxx out before we retire, the ducks cling to the shore and seem to be on guard of what awaits in the darkness. The toads are out in mass croaking. The larger birds walk the waterline, ready to strike. I hear the call of birds in the distance—a raucous honk or two from the Egyptian Goose. I have no idea

where the squirrels and iguanas are. I know not where
Hazel's warren is, but I hope they are all safe.

Final Phase

My passion attacks
itself, molten, never content
with what is crucial but
awed with the colors of
dwindling self-images.

I blend with downpours,
seeping into tributaries of worlds
mesmerized by languages never
heard.

I am called from dreams, besieged by
questions I can only answer at dawn, but I
am asleep then.

Of Course, the Clouds are Swollen

A landscape is like a beautiful piano piece,

awaking our emotions,

quieting our mind,

and making us dream.

We place ourselves in the distance,

near a small field

between the large sycamore trees

on the path that leads to the faraway hills.

We smile- because, whatever our age,

youth and summer are forever valued.

A place with a hold over us,

a place to linger.

A place to reach for another's hand.

On this pleasant yellow wall, my mind takes in the view.

The foreground has tall grass, wooed by a slight breeze,

with trimmed hedges encircling fragrant flowers.

Our nostrils fill with lilac, honeysuckle, and gardenia

on our path to the cottage.

There is a blue lake at the edge,

mostly out of sight.

White swans float as gulls drift above them

and songbirds

dash across the land.

Of course, the white clouds are swollen

slightly blocking the sun

still, you can feel the warmth

not only on you

but within you.

Our eyes search for a flaw,

because thoughts need redemption.

Uncomprehending that indulgence,

for a mixture of allure and delight

arises only

when nature, through art

speaks to us.

From this canvas to another,

one full of symbolism, framed in very dark reds.

Broodish and anticipating a harsh cold,

Autumn laments its sudden awakening to winter.

The foreground has

two strong yoked oxen, muscles strained,

their faces contorted

as they attempt to pull a plow whose tiller

is wedged between boulders.

The brawny male figure way to the left

is predominantly concealed by the hindquarters of the
animals.

With strength fading, his face lacks sentiment, yet he
prevails.

Large black birds rest on the barren branches

of elm trees in the background.

We feel helpless,

uneasy

because

there is no escape

from expectation.

Next is a large picture window,

the view is of nothing,

nothing in all its dull grayness.

Nothing is its everydayness.

I will never understand

why we let the filth of daily duplicity

permeate our souls

and lock the beauty of landscapes

away

in stodgy galleries.

Michelangelo's work Surrounds me, as does the Meaning of Plato's Words

*Rachel Carson, "The Sea Around Us," Staples Press, USA 1953

*Herman Hesse, "Steppenwolf," S. Fisher Verlag A. G. Berlin 1927

Thoughts Before the Story

I am void of being.

Not that I do not exist-

I do not relate to time.

I am in the dark, but not in the darkness.

My mind and body are delicately unraveling

*to become an ethereal sound wandering within a mood,
moving along and flowing.*

*Michelangelo's work surrounds me, as do the meaning of
Plato's words.*

*The ingenuity of Beethoven and Rodin meld together
into a mélange.*

Creativity and imagination devour me.

*I am journeying beyond color, beyond shape, beyond
nature,*

even beyond the outermost edges of beyond itself.

I catch sight of myself alongside the Faun in Debussy's
musical poem,

> *and I repeat to myself, "Is there anything more*
> *significant than art?"*

The Story

Today, there is a warm breeze

across a field of tall red and yellow flowers.

I can see the lake in the background.

At the end of the dirt path is a small cottage.

Inside there is one room, textured in outdated
undertones.

Once there were many hardcover books

in a large bookcase against a wall

next to a dilapidated leather couch.

Those old books with that old book smell,

most pages brown spotted,

pictures faded, written with difficult

old-fashioned words in French and English.

There were novels, biographies, art, geography,
philosophy, history, architecture,

astronomy, marvels of the world, and a number about
the sea.

The walls were lined with yellowing maps.

I always return to my memories; I gratefully unlace the
pleasurable.

She and I met here many summers ago.

Both of us were disappointed in our self-perception.

One of her first questions,

"Could transitory objects

be considered art?"

I had no idea what she meant.

Her voice was warm, and her large eyes were brown,

she always wore

a white blouse with navy slacks.

She was older than I, the last generation older,

the time of crooners and jazz.

As a night nurse, she read while her patients slept.

I think she had read every book in that cottage,

and I enjoyed her telling me about each one.

On the last day of summer, she told me to meet her that
evening

and bring a copy of my favorite book.

I brought Hesse- "*Steppenwolf.*"

The air was smoky as I approached.

She was in the yard, with a book in her hand

Every time she finished a page or so,

she tossed them into a wild bonfire.

After a few beers, she gave me

Rachael Carson's *"The Sea Around Us."*

I recited,

*"The sea is blue because the sunlight is reflected back to
our eyes from the water molecules or from very minute
particles suspended in the sea. In the journey of the light
rays downward into the water and back to our eyes, all
the red rays of the spectrum and most of the yellow have
been absorbed, so it is chiefly the cool, blue light that we
see."* *

When I finished, she read from *Steppenwolf,*

*"A wild longing for strong emotions and sensations
seethes in me, a rage against this toneless, flat, normal,
and sterile life. I have a mad impulse to smash*

something, a warehouse, perhaps, or a cathedral, or
myself, to commit outrages, to pull off the wigs of a few
revered idols..."

I knew what she wanted me to do, but I was hesitant

until she said,

"Retain never possess."

I remembered her first words to me.

"Are we all

not transitory objects?"

I never saw her again; I heard she moved to Barbados,

where she read while the island slept.

After the Story

I have never found a suspension between art and life.

The words, pictures, and sounds of all art

are no longer outside of me.

There is martyrdom in belief,

a quietness that comforts the soul.

I am in the light, but not the illumination,

Creativity and imagination have devoured me.

Philip Butera

I am beyond color, beyond shape, beyond nature,

even beyond the outermost edges of beyond itself.

The Fox Runs from the Hounds and the Gladiators Awake

I watch for openings,

bobbing and weaving

glancing,

here, there,

waiting for an opportunity.

I block a left,

but a right catches me.

Up against the ropes,

I cry, laugh

and ask God why,

words accuse

but rarely defend.

The next night

your sarcasm

only makes me want you more,

to un-pretend all

that is choreographed.

Your past lovers cling.

They have become gilded images,

phantoms that undress you,

while I

make drinks.

Bongos and congas,

fill the room

those loud island rhythms,

that glaze memory.

While you make love

to legends

with visions of conquests,

I untie the tides.

Waves roar and pound.

As warrior angels

search the shoreline

for outcasts,

lost maidens

beckon.

After the final round,

no flurries or distinction

just a

unanimous decision.

With my heart filled with misgivings

you shout to the audience,

"Love is what makes lovers lose."

The fox runs from the hounds,

and the gladiators awake.

I realign my gaze,

colors reign,

reds on fire, blistering yellows,

and sad

indifferent whites.

Contemplating love and fame,

I realize

the conversation we had long ago

about constellations

radiant with sublime affirmations,

remains a place,

we have never been.

Some Friends are Black Mirrors

Some friends are black mirrors

smiling a mournful smile,

distant from an artist's appeal.

They are indistinguishable in caskets

afraid to applaud expression

and salute

the opulence of fearlessness.

That simple cohesion

that warms a room

icily irritates the frowning resentful.

As a presence curves imagination

for images to roam within,

black mirrors,

elude to pretentiousness,

attempting to ring desire

with a caprice of influence.

But,

oceans roar,

owls watch, wolves chase

and stars are never

an afterthought,

Careful about choosing words,

I distance myself

from shadows undeserved.

I cling steadfastly to creativity

and prefer possibilities

to banality.

Glaring at the obvious

those with glassed frowns

entrenched in literalism

seethe from

abstraction.

I willingly

board the train without a destination,

and welcome the disorder

of originality.

I leer

at the melancholy hordes of sameness

and despise

the refrain of majorities

that

clasp tightly to contrition.

I tumble with acuity,

drink in hand,

bare breasts against my chest,

in a theatre of

dreams and sensuality.

Long ago,

when

nightfall

promised

imaginative encounters,

I vaulted through a black mirror

and

discovered my reflection

applauding me

on

becoming myself.

When a Dragon Blocks my Way

Two black and two buttermilk horses

pull my chariot through the bull ring.

The matador seems bewildered

as I unexpectedly

lead the bleeding animal out of the arena

to a green pasture,

where he runs on a path between the walnut trees to a

peaceful blue lake.

He steeps himself into the wetness, cooling his wounds.

After a time, he asks my horses if love is power.

The horses thrash the water,

and the wildest of them

states,

"Memory is an illusion, and reality is instinct."

I am a Knight, muscular, and ready.

The lords say I must search for the Grail,

but I know if found,

the world would become more sedate and obedient.

When dragons block my way, I never raise my sword.

I show them my copy of Plato's Republic.

They usually breathe fire, then relax and remark,

"The unjust grow wealthy by injustice."

When I speak to them about innocence and idealism,
they laugh,

sighting the greatest accomplishment of man

is his ease at betrayal.

During the Crusades, I wore

neither The Crescent Moon nor the Cross.

I struggled against time in perpetual moral discomfort.

At an oasis, I met an ass who was tutoring a young camel.

The ass who was conversant in history

told me that realities

are seldom interpreted by our minds.

The young camel,

whose eyesight was poor,

sighed,

"Some things exist regardless of our interpretation."

When I awoke,

I found the Crusaders had put the ass on a spit,

for they were hungry.

The young camel's legs collapsed

because her load was unbearable,

so she was clubbed to death.

I realized as I dug a grave to bury bones and body

there are limits to our knowledge

for if

we were noble,

both animals would still be discovering,

aware of the sun's warmth

and the moon's light.

In a large city with a dormant psychosis

while the art in a grand museum overawes,

I am told to produce my identification.

I recite a poem,

and a card stating

I was a sailor.

I follow them to an interrogation room

where they produce a photo of me reading

Sophocles and Zola.

I am asked to assess the morality of a consequence.

Should it be based on what we believe would happen

or what actually happens?

I answer sarcastically,

"How would the restoration engineers

like me to respond?"

There is no laughter before a public execution.

I hear in the wind,

Jean-Paul Marat was murdered,

Socrates was forced to drink hemlock,

and Christ crucified.

Why should I, an admirer of art,

be pardoned?

I imagine the rolling breakers

in a sublime Turner seascape

before answering,

"If Thomas Aquinas proved the existence of God,

and God is just,

then I am but a reservoir

of the information- I have gathered

from his goodness."

Some have witnessed how lethal, dangerous

and freeing a thought can be.

Others have knelt at the trough- not because they are

frightened,

but because they have children to protect.

I sit between

Oedipus Explaining the Enigma of the Sphinx,

and *Bacchanal of the Andrians*

contemplating Byron's words about Tasso,

"Long years of outrage, calumny, and wrong, and wrong;

Imputed madness, prison'd solitude,

And the mind's canker in its savage mood."

An elder raven who once taught law approaches.

He states,

"You have no defense.

The intolerant dismiss the existence of poetry,

declaring words have little basis.

In reality,

and contemporary truth is perception

corrected."

Because virtue has no intrinsic value,

an Officiant offers me a choice

of choosing

the mind or body.

I remember

my mother's smile

and have an identical epiphany

as a child

when he first smells

the fragrance of Lilacs.

The Silence, when it Shattered

The moonlight whitens the frost

above the snow on my window.

Icicle daggers lengthen.

The world is cold,

cold and indifferent.

You threw your glass

into the chandelier

and the embellishments,

shattered on the tile.

Your eyes said it all.

Hatred is

more profound than love.

We disregarded the certainty before the fall.

The escalated sarcasm fueled by alcohol,

and passion wringing its way to sex.

Just something,

anything

to wash us clean from each other.

Then the thunderous silence.

How simple,

I remain- you are gone.

Sad ballads, old photographs,

and phantom obsessions.

Regret is so cruel,

never letting a wound heal.

Always digging deeper,

expecting the end, discovering

a carousel endlessly circling,

all those animals

with frozen faces,

all in pain.

As winter gave way to early spring,

and the ice sheets on Lake Erie were breaking apart,

I met a woman.

She was dancing in the light rain, missing some puddles,

kicking up the water on others.

She had dark hair, dark eyes

and wore clothes suited for warmer weather.

She smiled at me.

> *I was not interested, not interested at all*
> *until I thought of you.*
> *I thought of all the thoughts I have had of you,*
> *I thought about how exhausting sorrow can be.*

In a bar with a large window overlooking the lake
watching gulls and finches
I told her I had lost time.
She laughed, saying,
"Didn't you know ladders have no handrails,
so falling is expected."

Another of the Greatest Fallen Angels

I was in the next room,

watching lines of cocaine disappear

when an entertainer asked if I had met you.

I found my way to your circle.

You were in sumptuous white,

exposing enough to encourage expectations.

The walls were decorated

with social portraitist paintings,

curvy women among the merchant class.

How comfortably you fit.

A beautiful white lotus

among the ravenously predatory.

Memories ago,

when abstraction

and analysis were avant-gardes,

we were lovers.

After-glow, revolutionaries,

mutineers

poured from sweet red wine.

You were my palette

when all the most imaginative

words came to mind.

And when my sentences needed an exclamation mark,

you unbuttoned your blouse.

I followed you into the gambling room.

The walls were lively,

with artwork focused on Zeus

and his many masquerades to seduce women.

I sat next to you,

and all your cards were gratifying,

while mine were transparent.

I learned from you

that knowledge and truth

hold

no virtue over illusions,

when courage and cunning are necessary.

Your playful eyes viewed this paradise lost,

dismissing any limitations.

Wasn't it Beatrice,

who,

after guiding Dante through

the nine celestial spheres of heaven,

sighed, *"Only pain can make life meaningful?"*

Then again,

pain is existential.

Maybe a consequence concerning expressions

drifting too close to certainty.

Eliminate temptations,

and there is no reason to gamble.

We are left alone to think,

to calibrate

conditions for violating taboos.

You joked, *"When pleasure is the only thing of value*

does the wanting dismiss the knowing?"

120

Your image is a reality in me,

a place to expose dreams.

When I added pressure, the glass burst in my hand,

"Cries and Whispers" came to mind.

That Bergman movie you thought tedious,

but I watched intently.

There is no evidence that eternity

can bring incarnations

of what

feelings insist are true.

When all is arbitrary,

revelations contradict

what is unrecognizable,

doors close,

and we step from the problematic

into the unknown.

I observed you leave with a cunning financier,

a collector of finery.

You took his arm

as if it were the combination

to a vault yet to be opened.

As realization became understanding,

I found myself on the patio

leaning against a marble column,

with a glass of champagne in my bandaged hand.

A slender redhead

in mint green with glassy blue eyes

was staring beyond the stars.

I asked the passing entertainer who she was.

There was pity in his voice,

"Another of the greatest fallen angels."

Philip Butera

So Many Footprints in the Sand

I ran to

Lady Chatterley,

she was in the arms of her lover.

Lady Macbeth,

is mad, but not for the love of me.

Lady Godiva cut her hair,

Madame Bovary expects too much,

Moll Flanders drinks,

Electra,

prefers to cry at the tombs of the dead,

Desdemona eloped,

Dulcinea is preoccupied with a quest

and

Guinevere never looks my way.

I am pieces of dreams,

lost in delusions

knowing how women,

real or imaged

bewitch me.

I cling, like a vine

to gestures, words,

and

eyes that linger.

I will always

be searching,

wanting,

waiting for the door to open

skirts to sway,

buttons to unbutton,

and fate,

to play a smooth melody

so I can present a line

and

watch *that* smile break.

So many footprints in the sand,

stars counted,

amusement parks,

candles lit,

bedrooms approached,

Philip Butera

breasts kissed

and

times

suspended

between

anticipation

and expectation.

Searching for Identity

Immerse yourself in this space of imagination,

full of dazzling colors and wondrous words.

Don't leave; stay there,

and words will find you.

We will be a musical composition,

sweet and poised with exquisite thrills.

With arms enveloping each other,

nude and defiant,

we will step from the precipice.

If the depth of thought is infinity,

we will shine on the other side of what can be known,

signing autographs as consummate sculptors of life.

Of course,

we will be envied by the innocent

who sport serried smiles as they shuffle mindlessly

from this moment

until bedtime,

unaware corporate bandits have stolen their souls.

Of course,

we will be hated by the affluent

who have spent their lives outraged

that legal pads have lines

to consider alternatives.

They bellow hysterically- plenty is never enough.

Of course,

like all who know the truth, we will be loathed.

Because declaring

we are all born racing toward death

searching for identity

clawed by our own

self-deception,

is a nuance

experienced

yet never staged.

I am an author,

with a

scalpel in my hand.

I create prose,

while

imagination creates me.

I revere nakedness

because

I know God is a gambler

who lost his virginity in a brothel

of his own making.

All things lyrical to the divinities

are insufferable to the artless

who slog away to make

margins broader and broader

till there is no space

left to breathe.

I am a poet,

loathing those without a conscience.

I have never needed permission,

so I have never lied.

We see nothing till

we understand it

and when we do

every imitation must be discarded

Philip Butera

and every

cold heart pierced.

I am a playwright

conjuring a new world.

Expunging

this comic farce

where money enthusiasts, without repentance,

sword in hand

slash

and slay

wanting

what is beyond

more and

more

The Reflection from a Million Mirrors Shattering

Introduction

Long past and far away
I came for me.
I had this fever with
unimaginable imaginings
of me
of every me.
For I am but the reflection
from a million mirrors shattering,
blessed and cursed.
Incompatible with nuance
confused by misunderstanding
I cannot find my way,
yet I have come to realize what is,
is not
and with gentle sadness,
I fear I cannot be.
What is sculptured from marble,
painted on canvass,

or notes on paper

are but a misty bewilderment.

As cacophonies swirl about me

and falling Angels

unfamiliar to themselves

simmer in the distance

I grasp contradiction,

unhinged within

an enigma.

One

Eclipsed by inconsistency,

where do I flee?

Prometheus, his biceps bulging,

calls to me, "She will see you now."

Then with a sorrowful grin, he adds, "I wish you luck."

I never move,

nevertheless, I am traveling,

fumbling through existence,

everything reappears before it appears.

I stumble away from a claustrophobic fury

and find myself on a peaceful shore,

warm with satisfying waves.

I shout to the sun to stay above me,

bathe me in nourishment,

but my voice is corralled before execution.

The sun becomes the moon, the shoreline

a flowering valley between high peaks.

The wind brings on a chill.

Nothing has meaning, just insistence,

a persistent drum pounds without remorse.

Wrapped into circles, circling, I plod through awareness.

Daffodils, buttercups, and marigolds cushion my fall.

I always wanted to be where

I was going,

beyond thought, beyond thinking,

beyond what is where essence

and madness dissolves.

Two

False images allure,

as metaphors slither,

but they are swept away by a cavalier vibrancy

from a cascading sky.

Visions spy me, uncovering all pretense.

I am getting nearer

to where there is only stillness.

The voice I hear is familiar.

Above me, on a cloud made of Italian textures,

my father enjoys

what he has forgotten he desired.

He cannot see me; I am unknown to him.

I am an impression of myself,

a clue about to be revealed.

The crack of thunder sounds,

yet the bright blue sky remains silent.

Nothing has a voice, and what can be understood

is unknowable,

because the astuteness needed,

that delicate, varied, and dimensional

aliveness is still

evolving from a dream.

Three

Charon, the ferryman across the river Styx,

asks me to board.

His emotions are alive on another's face.

He looks past

what is

to what must be.

With large muscular arms on his oar,

he says, "Justice is a human creation."

As he hands me a two-headed

black and yellow lizard,

he quips,

"I use her to navigate the unfolding of hypocrisy."

Four

Thetis, the future mother of Achilles,

tells me

as she has defended Zeus,

she will guide me into the domain

I most covet to be.

Her breasts are heavy, and I begin to drink

She is all women, known and desired by me.

When I have consumed my fill, she wipes my mouth,

swallows the lizard, and spreads her long legs.

All mythology is a concept I am creating.

Thetis' vaginal lips bring me inside her,

the warm moistness blesses me.

There is no absence within her womb,

and benevolent sleep

lasts before time

and after existence.

My journey has begun.

Five

DaVinci is lying back, his hands behind his head.

He is envisioning Camus writing, "L'Etranger."

He gazes at me,

then sits up, asking, "Are you the one who knows why?"

I am mystified at the sprinkling of actual thought

permeating our presence.

Naked and alive without any encumbrance,

I ask, "Am I here?"

Philip Butera

His laughter is so loud,

long, and innocent,

small birds gather within

and make nests.

They chirp without fear of being,

and their song develops

into a theme Mozart would capture.

Finally, after several stars become

languid moments of belief,

he responds,

"No, Plato's forms are yet to have boundaries."

Torches appear,

and poetic words determine my direction.

Venus, on a swing,

glides past above me.

I try to reach for her,

but I am forgotten.

She melts into the skyline,

an illusory dreaminess

tinged with impending storms.

Six

In me,

not that me,

but this me

defined by a perfectionistic ideology for being

fills my curious persona.

"It is time," laments DaVinci.

Prometheus puts the dice in my mind,

and into my hand.

All love affairs come to mind,

all triumphs come to mind,

reason comes to mind.

Expressionless faces stare,

mythological figures, fictional characters

and Gods in their finery,

relentless in their depth

circle quotation marks yet to be written.

There is nothing,

not even gloom,

yet I am conspicuous.

Seven

No sounds are heard,

though sad music plays,

a dirge full of expectancy.

Sjöfn, Nordic goddess of love, nude and seductive

demands I kneel.

Wrapping her legs tightly around my neck,

she places her sword at my lips.

Irrational within a paradox,

a dispute about myself spills from a rhapsody

into an inquisitional quandary.

The crowd does not appear

in an arena

that does not exist,

yet the roar remains, "Roll the dice,"

and the eyes of Prometheus become flames.

Eight

The dice tumble,

tumble, and turn.

They bounce.

Dots are lines

dots are blurs,

dots are deciders.

Hera leads the procession,

Aphrodite follows.

One die twirls, the other winds around,

the shouting is frenzied.

Sjofn,

so blonde, so fair,

so perfect, so icy

just giggles,

a tinkling, devilish snicker,

as nightfall overtakes darkness,

and nightmares overtake dreams.

The dice roll, they roll.

I confess I am nameless.

Rainbows of words cloud my view.

That is when I realize

I will forever be wandering within a storm,

this two-fisted tempest

 and the next,

and the next.

Philip Butera

Nine

Athena,

understanding complexity is a pleasure,

never a burden

immediately removes the numbers from the dice.

A herd of magnificent multicolored mares gallops past.

They blend into an abstraction-

a painting, a symphony, and a poem.

Everything past is a memory of the future.

Ten

Charon's ferry slowly leaves the cold waters

for the negative after-image of eternity

while

my lizard

crawls from the soft womb of Thetis.

It has another head,

red, cerise,

crimson, cinnamon cherry.

This head devours the others,

and the lizard,

now furious about its demise

digs its claws into my thoughts.

And I,

uncertain about my self-awareness

but knowing

imagination is reason

courting fantasy,

disappear.

Poems
by
Philip M. Butera
and
Lorna Thomson

Languid Moments
By Philip Butera and Lorna Thomson

You once spoke these words to me,

"I will never lie to you."

and,

I know this to be true.

Still,

you are

the most significant lie - the secret - of my life.

I watch you,

not trusting a breath

to escape.

An imprecise beat

of my heart

catapulting calamity.

All movement is sensual,

and I am transposed.

Oh,

languid moments

of invincible youth.

I watch you during

random moments,

your idle acts,

foolish endeavors

and serious instances.

Each movement

re-scarring the reminder

that you are miles away,

with many reminiscences now layered upon

those times in classrooms, pubs, and beds.

I see you,

where waves receive the shoreline.

Where there is meaning to

precious visions

of all things delicately-colored

and Rodrigo is heard as you make your way

to someplace the sun's rays

give the perfect contrast

of light and shadow

to paint your lover.

She is nude and complements the ocean's impatience,

while I

remain a faraway occurrence

behind the horizon's curtain

of my lies.

In a fresh food market,

I am deciding whether to buy

Fuji or Delicious apples,

though many recipes for pie

recommend Granny Smith,

when an old friend approaches.

It has been years.

Her hair was once long and blonde,

now between rust and chestnut,

hugging her still attractive face.

Our conversation takes us to the wine bar

where one name leads to another.

I mention you, and she contends

straightforwardly,

you were handsome but indifferent in bed.

"Funny," she says, "I ran into him

at an airport a few years back.

His bravado remained but

he confessed he was

a failure at everything,

even love."

On the table is a knife.

I pick it up and began to stab her,

I cannot stop.

No one is allowed

to jostle my fantasies,

no one.

As I leave her to bleed out,

I think of you,

sunning yourself,

editing your words

for a new poetry book.

A young woman looking

much like me when I was young,

is at your side.

Her breasts are firm

and tanned.

You kiss her pink nipples

from time to time to

encourage your creativity.

Once home, I undress,

view my image in a full-length mirror

and sneer,

"Never stop lying to me."

Ruptured Canopies
By Philip Butera and Lorna Thomson

A trapeze artist

preens

before mirrors,

her breasts scarred from falls

and mistaken steps.

The handsome magician,

drink in hand,

rummages through

life's deceptions.

I juggle

cotton candy dreams

with

sugar waffle fantasies.

I am safe,

in a hatbox

among the elephants and the lions.

Confused,

by crowds hurrying to see

and those

rushing to leave.

There is suspicion between art and life,

which is more accurate?

Hugging the curb of want,

I have a razor's edge

view of fate,

a tapestry of spreading shadows,

woven with brandished egos

and profound fear.

Time to move,

time to shake off the numbness of bad luck

and missed opportunities

against the dark of the world.

I look around me, not wide-eyed,

but cautiously aware

calamities are paradoxes

swelled with inconveniences.

Paper plates, cups, and torn balloons
are strewn about.

Flies and other insects

swarm on the decaying food.

The heavy air

heats the remains of liquid in discarded bottles.

Mosquitoes swell,

while toads contemplate their next moves.

I notice wheels from broken strollers,

dirtied diapers,

and abandoned plastic products,

all scattered on the dry, dusty ground.

And everywhere that stench of trash,

of garbage,

of things sweet and sticky

tossed away.

Appetites crave more.

And more indicates

an unappeasable desire.

Thick ropes on large poles

are loosened,

tents collapse and

restlessness permeates,

Philip Butera

reverberating through the animal cages.

There are no more illusions.
The high wires have disappeared.
The thrills have become thoughts
lost in the distance.
The mesmerization
of magic and mysteries
has faded.

Life is a hammer
pounding on an anvil,
and all the ruptured canopies
must be mended
before the next show.

A Circus of Mirrors

By Philip Butera and Lorna Thomson

I need you

to recognize me

as the continuum

becomes a circle

that belongs to us.

I beg you to applaud

my fearful courage

pushing past the shrouds of now

into

the light of us.

I wander through

a spectacle of mirrors

knowing I am a symbol

of constant restraint.

Philip Butera

                    Panic

              hastens my breath

                    and

                  assaults

                my thoughts.

          I remain in a departure

        of endless contemplation

        and though seduction

            seems available,

              my obsession

            never elevates.

Lost,

in a soft, red, leather chair,

legs extended and spread,

children in their rooms,

magazine on my lap,

and white wine in my hand

all escape

is quelled.

I am a Consummate Gardener

Philip Butera and Lorna Thomson

I am a consummate gardener,

living without pretense.

I dig,

pull out clover,

pull out weeds,

but I let stones remain.

Stones, tell me how I have gardened.

They ask to be touched.

I rub them between my fingers,

feel the caked dirt,

and listen to their stories.

They lie, though.

They want to please

so they

complement desires.

My big brown dog, bright-eyed,

and unphased by dirty, muddy, or wet paws,

never travels far from me.

I unleash her,

but she never strays.

She is content to be my archangel,

while I do all the spading, weeding,

transplanting, trenching, scraping,

with few tools and without a smile.

Every time I step into this garden,

like Sisyphus, my perpetual punishment continues.

Squirrels conspire with birds to distract me.

Occasionally, I uncover the small bones of their relatives.

Now and then, I find what they have buried.

But most times, I poke, plow, and think

about the absurdity of gardening

and the futility of being successful at it.

My neighbors scoff at me.

They have no spirited dog nor dismissive cat.

Their trees are tall,

and professionals tend full leafy bushes.

They are a distant couple

who spend no time outside their thoughts,

self-absorbed with moral decay;

they measure time by what is possessed.

Better to harvest treasure with false conviviality

then dig and unearth shards of sharp objects

that cut and disfigure.

Wasps and bees circle, dart, and linger.

If they are annoyed, they will sting.

Blister beetles, if ingested accidentally

or incidentally, can cause death.

Orange and black monarch butterflies

warn they are toxic, and

toads never fail to startle me.

The larger animals; muskrats, moles, and raccoons

make their presence known

as the moon rises,

when I am dining, sinning, or reading

about gardening.

No matter how pleasing,

there is no music,

that can be appreciated while your hands

are going deeper into the darkness.

It is no secret,

the earth's blackness is an uncompromising foe,

indifferent

to all things living.

The sun sneers, and the clouds darken,

winds race to find me, the moisture from the lake

picks up the dust and sprays my face.

I am an addict, single-minded

with one purpose.

I acknowledge that.

There are no distractions

just restless

Philip Butera

absurdity.

I wear no knee pads,

no protective covering,

no gloves.

I dislike hats.

And I hate when I feel sweat and dirt

glide down my back.

I am never satisfied

with what I am accomplishing.

But that has little to do with gardening.

My dog

sniffs the exhumed soil,

and,

as I twist my hands

to seize what is deeper,

I realize

I have underestimated the potential

of gardening,

like

I have underestimated

the potential

of my own

curiosity.

A Rush of Emotions and Nakedness

by Philip Butera and Lorna Thomson

She:

I have written to you

a thousand times,

but my words

cannot find the page.

Sometimes,

I call your name

and surprise myself

by the sound of it.

I have

thought about phoning

but the conversation

I want to have

is the conversation

we can never have.

I remember us in bed somewhere,

not much conversation

just a rush of emotions

and nakedness.

I liked the way you felt

against me.

I liked the way

we fit.

I liked so many things

back then

and I surmised

all would be mine.

He:

I saw a recent photo of you,

we still have mutual friends.

Your blue eyes are bright,

and your shape never gives away

you are the mother of two,

grandmom of one.

We used to drink to merriment,

to pleasure

and all of its challenges.

We laughed

while discussing psychology

and music.

We used to do so many things,

But none involved

the times to come.

The webs of my life,

though tattered, still,

reach back to those days.

To that movie theatre

where my hand moved up your leg

to your inner thigh

and you magically became

naked under your dress.

I have traversed

the times between then and now,

telling a million stories about

voyages and mishaps.

I've been to places

where my swagger

was challenged,

so

I slipped out of sight

into the neverland of

being myself.

She:

I know

the choices I have made,

my domesticity

being

carefully

crafted with

silk and flannel.

But

my life

has always been textured

with

presumption

and

I make no apologies

for the near

misses.

Her & Him:

It seems

we have always

been seduced by the model

in our minds.

Even now

we undress the days

and

tell ourselves

the deceits

we need to hear.

Philip Butera

When She Asked
By Lorna Thomson and Philip Butera

Icy webs etched on windowpanes

keep the cold at bay.

If there is another time around

do you think we could get it right?

Held in crosshairs,

conscience abandons her post.

Jeering,

her misgivings tossed at nightfall

plummeting,

without celebration,

into the dark, dark mysteries

pending.

We both know,

if then were now

and moments, lulls, and sways

would return,

we would

remain, naked lovers,

twined in silhouette,

dancing away

from all

that

kept us apart.

Peeking Past the Sharp Edges of Now
By Lorna Thomson

Readying to look,

preparing to dare,

questions linger, if only delusions.

Inquisitiveness more than

self-deceit.

Yet,

peeking past the sharp edges of now,

those taunting edges

of disregard

loom.

I am terrified to be seen,

and broken

that I will not be noticed.

I have something inside me,

a refrain

from distant dreams

and

Philip Butera

faded lovers

that clash

with those defiant naked women

on trapezes

in my mind.

I know the ladies you have bedded,

beautiful and resilient,

strutting like Aphrodite,

unconcerned

by all they convey.

I envy their arrogance

and despise them

for all

that I am not.

My desire for you

remains a constant

in a lifetime

of uncertainties.

A reminder of choices made

and dominoes tumbled

from memories that linger,

re-coloring a sepia landscape,

sensual violet, bright orange

and vibrant blues.

Just teach me how to connect the stars,

so I can glide past the mundane,

undress the moon,

dance in the tides

and

navigate the night,

singing

while I fly away.

With no Destination
By Lorna Thomson

The crowded elevator

travels up, up,

up,

emptying those preoccupied with purpose.

A small girl with curious blue eyes

is the last to exit.

I am alone,

continuing to ascend.

The door rattles open,

icy winds and swirling snow

greets me.

I sense rather than see.

The storm is overwhelming.

Resignation creeps

upon me

as the elevator disappears,

leaving no trace of its existence.

With no destination,

uncertain

and without direction

I step.

With each move

I sink deeper into the snow.

Sky and horizon

blend into a shapeless,

white screen.

A distantly

remembered voice

interrupts the blindness.

An image,

just out of reach.

A young woman,

imagined but true,

comes my way.

Every

chaotic white moment

becomes another.

Philip Butera

The aimless snow whirls

about us,

without form or regard,

restless yet sublime.

I trudge further

into

cold uncertainty,

and from

the icy opaqueness,

my curious blue eyes

indelicately surrender

to the

bleakness

of my

unforgiving dreams.

Biography

Philip M. Butera grew up in Buffalo, NY, earned a BS degree From Gannon College in Erie, PA, served in the US Navy then received an MA in Psychology from Simon Fraser University in Vancouver, Canada. He has published four books of poetry, "Mirror Images and Shards of Glass," "Dark Images at Sea," "I Never Finished Loving You," "Falls from Grace, Favor and High Places," and one crime novel, "Caught Between." His second novel, "Art and Mystery: The Missing Poe Manuscript," will be published in Fall 2021. He has a column in the quarterly magazine Per Niente. and was a contributing editor for EatSleepWrite.net. Philip won full scholarships to the 2017 Palm Beach Poetry Festival, 2017 Creative Capital Workshops, and the 2018 Creative Capital Advanced Weekend Workshop. The Cultural Council of Palm Beach premiered his play, "The Apparition," and exhibited his poetry. The Artists Guild Gallery/Boca Raton Museum of Art also presented "The Apparition." Philip is the publicity coordinator for Mystery Writers of America - Florida Chapter. He lives in Boynton Beach, Florida, and is on Facebook. His e-mail address is Terracelanegroup@gmail.com.

The Art Box Gallery of St. Augustine, Fl, will present a live performance of "The Apparation," Fall of 2021.

Philip Butera

7StoryRabbit Audiobooks and Jacol Publishing will collaborate on a radio production of "Caught Between" to be aired in early 2022.

You can read more of Phil's work at www.jacolpublishing.com

www.ingramcontent.com/pod-product-compliance
Lightning Source LLC
Chambersburg PA
CBHW070013110426
42741CB00034B/1518